THE
RESURRECTION
OF
THE
SNAILS

NICHOLAS RINALDI

THE RESURRECTION OF THE SNAILS

and other poems

JOHN F. BLAIR, PUBLISHER
Winston-Salem, North Carolina

Copyright © 1977 by Nicholas Rinaldi
Library of Congress Catalog Card Number: 77–13798
All rights reserved
ISBN 0–89587–002–9
ISBN 0–910244–97–9 pbk.
Printed in the United States of America
by Heritage Printers, Inc.
Charlotte, North Carolina

Library of Congress Cataloging in Publication Data

Rinaldi, Nicholas, 1934–
    The resurrection of the snails, and other poems.

    I,   Title.
PS3568.I47R4   811'.5'4   77–13798
ISBN 0–89587–002–9
ISBN 0–910244–97–9 pbk.

for JACQUELINE

ACKNOWLEDGMENTS

The author wishes to express his appreciation to the following publications for permission to reprint poems which have appeared or will appear in their pages:

Epoch for "Cabbages" and "Bliss."

Prairie Schooner for "It Happens," copyright © 1973 by the University of Nebraska Press, and "Consumer," copyright © 1972 by the University of Nebraska Press.

Arizona Quarterly for "Vermeer."

Poem #3–4 (Nov. '69) for "Quarrel" and #10 (Nov. '70) for "Pink Knickers."

Carolina Quarterly for "Museum."

New American Review for "Panther."

The Yale Review for "Horowitz Among the Lemon Trees," copyright Yale University.

The Literary Review (Summer '77 XX 4), published by Fairleigh Dickinson University, Madison, N.J., for "Goodbye" and "Overkill."

Ball State University Forum for "Hauling in the Nets."

CONTENTS

PART ONE

WAITING
ROOM

CABBAGES

I walk down Broadway, and all the skyscrapers are cabbages,
   big fists of leaves growing mountainously.
Once they were tall and slender, now they're round and
      green, all in neat rows.
Look close: you can see their slow movements as they grow.

We walk together, hand in hand, in and out among
the cabbages. This corner was a bus stop once,
but now the ants are busy, moving sand.
And here there was a subway, gophers live there now.
Stay with me a while under this blue, unfurling leaf—
here we can be alone, and from here we can see
   far down the avenue.

The traffic stands still, all the cars have put down roots.
Flowers push through the radiator grilles.
There is no noise now, only the slow quiet groans
   of the cabbages growing.

LIFEGUARD

They are leaping in the water like salmon,
    a hundred laughing girls,
wet hair falls dark across their faces.
Every day I watch them: their bodies turn brown,
splashing beyond the shoreline, strung out
like notes on a scale.
                    And now I save one:
where a hand jerks above the surface and disappears,
I plunge for a life and touch her loneliness.
She fights, turns, wrestles, twists—her body
rubs against mine,
my hands know all of her.
                    I draw her from the black water.
On the sand, she lies exhausted, a ruined word.
She doesn't smile. Her eyes go skyward,
staring
into blue emptiness.

HOROWITZ AMONG THE LEMON TREES

Loneliness of the valley of the unpruned lemon trees—
this is where Horowitz resides, waiting
for the moon to rise behind the dense foliage
of his feelings. Does he remember
how old his father was when he died, or why his mother,
on a summer afternoon, went laughing
in the garden behind the house, and threw her shoe
at a flock of crows? Was she thinking
of the black wings of flight, a lazy escape
into the blue sky of her memories?
He lingers in the valley, where the lemons hang,
small, dim lanterns, and knows
that he will never understand
why the crows flew off, leaving their shadows behind.
Such dismal, shabby shadows. He folded them
like tissue paper, keeping them
for some moment in the future, an occasion—
he didn't know when, or where, or why.

Is this the worst, he wonders.
Beyond these neglected trees, is there
no other terror waiting for him?
He picks a lemon and sinks his teeth
deep into the rind, getting the bitter taste.
Then lets the lemon fall.
Alone among the twisted trees, this
is what he knows: he could endure much more,
and—possibly—already has.

BURNING THE STAMPS

We burn the postage stamps—
the 2¢ Jefferson, the henna brown Martha Washington,
the NRA, the AEC, the $5 Alexander Hamilton.
Burn and burn: a slow, persistent fire.
George Washington rests a thoughtful finger on his chin.
"Yes," he confides, "I fell in love
with another man's wife, but did
no wrong—and that's as true
as any cherry." He lingers solemnly,
the piercing stare, the pockmarked face.
And then he flares, a sudden tongue of flame,
and blows off in the wind, a microscopic cinder.

OVERKILL

Kill all the swans, don't let any of them escape.
And the mallards, the pelicans—
let all the rivers run with their blood.

Shoot the pumpkins: fire pointblank.
When their orange roundness explodes to shattered nothing,
light your tongue with a match and sing.

Let none of the snapdragons live.
Bludgeon them to death with clubs—thrash wildly,
until their ruffled flowers are bruised and dead.

And now the apple trees, those old reminders
of a paradise we've never known. Strip off the bark,
grind up the leaves . . . bring on the flame throwers!

Well done, well done. Better than planned.
Enough for now.
Sleep. Rest. Get ready. Tomorrow, the frogs.

BLISS

Ah, to be on a Pacific Isle, spreading syphilis
and sin. Bring on the palm trees! Bring on
the brown-breasted girls! And then to be reformed by a
sex-starved female missionary, you.

You could have a bible in one hand, a first-aid kit
in the other. When the natives are sick,
you pass out band-aids. During a thunderstorm
you teach the medicine man how to sing: *Rock of Ages*
and *Nearer My God to Thee*. I want to sing too—
teach me. But all those pubescent girls,
with their brown smiles! You pray,
and urge me to become a vegetarian. In emergencies,
you practice minor surgery.

It's always summer, and usually it's fresh fish.
You long for sauerkraut, which you haven't had
for years. Through a mail order catalogue
I get you a Schwinn bicycle, a picture of the Grand
Canyon, and a year's supply of Tampax.
The ocean is mysterious with your green moods.

Maybe there will be cholera.
The natives die—how stiff their bodies!
We throw them on a pyre and burn the germs away.
Always we boil our water.

Life is difficult in the tropics,
it's easy to let things slide. Still, I do my best
to keep up appearances. I scrub the palm trees
with Clorox, and paint the coconuts yellow.
When you are sad, I cut flowers out of a magazine
and paste them on your door.

But what happened to the Chief Headsman,
the one whose appendix you removed? He died.
There is a funeral, with much dancing and wailing.
And then a burnt sacrifice: we are it.
While the flames curl up around our ankles,
I hold your hand. You thank me for the yellow coconuts,
I thank you for the aspirins. My eyes are on
the seven naked girls
who bring logs to the fire.

PINK KNICKERS

I sit on the stone fence
between the golf course and my house
and watch golfers like circus animals
browsing across the green:
blue hat, white shirt, pink knickers,
another in a yellow shirt and brown slacks—
one, two, three practice swings,
then swing again, this time meaning it,
and the small white ball nibbles across the grass,
and the yellow shirt and the pink knickers
disappear behind trees—

and I, sitting on the fence,
chase a golf ball the size of the sun
across hills and green grass, a tedious
journey through trees, in and out
of sandtraps. Beyond the hills
the sun dips low and burns
the grass into blades of blood.
I swing my club: one, two, three practice strokes
and memory bursts like a balloon full of confetti
and my father, wearing pink knickers,
stands on the edge of a hill,
eyes closed with concentration,
playing his violin.

     Father,
had you worn pink knickers,
your music might have laughed
more than it did, and you too might have laughed
more than you did—
for your soul's peace I resurrect you now
from the limbo of old age
and plant you in this crosseyed vision
to play and play, silhouette against the red sun,
drawing from silver strings

       the tonguetied laughter
of your browneyed soul.

THE PLANES ARRIVE

The planes arrive with cargos of flowers
   the pregnant bellies of the planes
bearing black narcissus from Nigeria
   orchids from Peru, carnations from anywhere
the planes fly over Manhattan
   dropping all their flowers
the flowers burn with an awesome beauty
   falling, burning lavishly
petals of orchids, petals of black narcissus
   a rare fragrance rises from the flames
the depots burn with the extravagance of dahlias
   the skyscrapers are trellises of fire
this fragrance, this incandescence
   violets of Uganda, bloodroot of Bangladesh
red rafflesias from Borneo
   it would never have been accomplished
if the planes were not arriving, and again arriving
   their improbable burden of flowers.

THE TAILORS WHO MAKE THE EMPEROR'S CLOTHES APOLOGIZE FOR THEIR MISTAKES & PROMISE TO DO BETTER IN THE FUTURE

We apologize for the long, the short, the tight
and the impossible. We've made mistakes.
We know the difference between
the true and the false, the firm and the uncertain.
No one is perfect.
We regret the slow, the stiff, and the brown.
We offer a refund for
the crooked and the dim. We try & try.
Over the years we've had our problems, but we
improve. We do well (generally) when left
to our own devices. Accept
our guarantee. We offer the splendor
of mystical translucence: garments woven from
the morning mist, a softness never imagined,
a coat the color of clear glass when it is
seen through. If you want
what we have in mind, you will have to wait,
dream, pray, & focus your desires. Give us time.
We have more to show
than you can ever hope   to see.

WAITING ROOM

Who are these people who gather in the doctor's office—
this woman with a wart on her nose, these two young girls
who play a music box and giggle, this old man
& his daughter . . . have they flown in from another continent
suffering from assorted maladies, rare diseases,
coming to this doctor
as the only one who can cure them? They have walked,
groped through a wilderness,
through regions infested with hostile aborigines,
across mountain ranges, deserts, raging rivers, pampas,
through the country of the head-hunters,
arriving here, slightly out of breath, with bruised feet.
The doctor is late. "Detained," the nurse explains.
We wait. The woman with a wart on her nose
reads a book. *She* waits. The two girls
play their music box. *They* wait. The old man
gazes emptily. *He* waits. The woman with leotards, sitting
opposite the old man, looks as if she might be good
at peeling off her clothes: first the skirt,
then the blouse, then the leotards . . .
The old man rises up from his infirmities, reaching, moaning.
His daughter restrains him. The woman with the wart
refuses to notice. The two girls play their music box.
How flawless she is, the lady in leotards
without her leotards . . . how like an apparition!
I wonder what improbable affliction
has brought her from so far away
to this moment in the doctor's office.

The old man rises up, rises up. The two girls giggle.
The nurse steps in, putting an end to all this
with a piece of bad news: the doctor has suffered
a coronary occlusion. We don't believe. She tells us
again. We still don't believe. We shuffle
out of the waiting room, amazed, annoyed, disgruntled,
having traveled from far-off countries, across pampas
and rivers, carrying our ailments, taking them
home again, down the elevator, into the traffic,
back to the dangerous regions of the snakes, the lizards,
and the poisoned water holes. The woman in leotards
hails a taxi. The old man & his daughter
drive off in a station wagon. The lady with the wart
gets my ear. "Such a thing," she says, meaning
anything at all. "Such a terrible,
terrible thing!"

TIME REVEALING ITSELF
IN THE SHAPE OF A TREE

Time is not what we imagined,
  we do what we can.
We paint time and watch it grow,
feed it the correct minerals.
Time is an enormous tree, we decorate it
with multicolored lights. We paint this tree
and nail strips of aluminum on it.
We cannot subtract this tree
or add it up,
or multiply it, or divide it into squares.
This tree is beyond our comprehension
yet we know (deeply) how important
it is: it is not the tree of knowledge, or the tree of life,
      or the tree of doubt, or the tree of night,
     or the tree of slow accumulation and debt,
but a tree with its own meaning, and it invites us
to go inside. We open a door
and walk in, astounded
by amber light. Our eyes
adjust slowly. There are stairs in this tree,
we climb and climb. The stairs lead
to the top, but the top grows away
as we move up. There are rooms in this tree,
windows where we linger, measuring the light
from decaying stars.

If we could get out of
this tree, we would. If this tree could be
cut down, we would have it done.
If it could be poisoned and made to die, we would buy
the chemicals.

The tree continues:
new leaves, new branches.
It grows & grows   and we are
locked in.

18

PANTHER

With Robert Mitchum I hunt the black cat.
Paw prints in the snow.
He's a big one, but Mitchum is tough.
The horse whinnies.
Indian Joe-Sam is scared.
The snow blows, flakes like silver dollars.

Diana Lynn waits at the house,
her dress buttoned up to her chin.
No one will see her breasts.
Her hair is braided in a bun.
She has the hots for young Harold.

Arthur, the middle brother, is killed—
clawed by the cat.
While Harold digs the grave, Ma lays him out proper.
There is a unicorn carved on the antique bedstead.
At the funeral, Ma throws dirt on the coffin.
Pa is drunk on whiskey.

Mitchum presses on.
I follow along, his shadow in the snow.
Look out for Mitchum: he is burly, crass, power mad.
But wise.
He knows who the panther really is:
". . . the cause of all the trouble in the world."
A pregnant pause.
"The evil in everybody."

Diana Lynn offers herself to Harold—
"You'll be alone with me, if I lead you by the hand."
He hesitates, then lays her down in the straw.
They don't take off their clothes.

In a cave, Mitchum lights a fire and reads Keats.
"When I have fears that I may cease to be . . ."
He does have fears—
when he finds the black panther, he runs.
Down the icy slopes of the Rockies.
Panic drives him.
He falls down a canyon.
Dies.

I know now who I am.
I am not Mitchum's shadow—
I am Harold in a mackinaw,
trudging across a mile of snow.
Behind a grove of pines, I shoot the black cat dead.
Diana Lynn is mine.

Joe-Sam has the last word:
"Him devil—black panther."
Ma smiles sweetly.
Pa will never drink again.

QUARREL

Don't frown, don't file your nails.
Look, love, if you want to be cross, there are better ways.
Here: throw this chair.

Yesterday we walked in the park, through a grove of pines.
Today we sit at home.
Have some wine, claret is best for a mood like this.

But now your eyes are glowing red plums.
You plunge your nail file
into my heart. Look at all my blood
on the kitchen floor! I pull out the nail file
and stab your eyes.

And now, in the yellow glare
of the kitchen lamp, we sip our claret—
you with your blind eyes, I with my bleeding heart.
All night long we drink
    and mumble our way toward morning.

HAULING IN THE NETS
OFF THE COSTA DEL SOL

Quickly but not without care
we gather in the wet, heavy nets
a big haul

so many small fish (slippery)
shine in the sun
dying splinters of silver

the sea is good
the man in the truck
waits

we sell these fish to him
for some pesetas, worn coins
bearing the face of Franco

we do not remember
the old war   choose
to put it aside

our clothes dry out on the sand
we will eat, tonight, paella
and drink the red wine of the region—

the big nets needing eight men
will be ready for us
tomorrow

ALTERNATIVE: BLUE

A blue tree, a blue afternoon
Blue leopards move dreamily in a field of blue grass
Soft blue, vague blue, unlikely blue
Blue in the manner of an elevator dropping ninety
    floors per minute toward a sudden upswirling stop
Blue colloids in blue flasks, moon rocks in blue museums
We are all blue, we will never be any other color
Our eyes are blue, our teeth are blue
Blue is something we wanted and achieved, we invented it
We wait in blue shadows in blue neighborhoods
Our sleep is blue
Blue is our freedom and our equality: we wished it, made it,
    mass-produced it, and passed it around
We print blue messages on blue paper, and from blue planes
    we drop these messages on dazed populations in far-off
        parts of the world: they watch, and wait, and wonder
Blue for memory, blue for things seen and slowly forgotten
Blue like the sound of a harmonica on a warm
    afternoon in September
Blue suburbs, blue mountains, blue thunderstorms
Blue in the shape of eucalyptus trees growing secretly
    in the dense landscape of our minds
Blue is our essential loneliness: we will die, we will
    not be found in the usual places
Blue is our meaning and our intransigence, our slow dream
Years after we are gone we will be remembered as a blue haze,
    a blue echo, a blue mood

We will linger in blue photographs in desolate rooms
Our voices will be heard on blue tapes
   played over and over again
We will be blue in libraries, thumbed and fingered by weary
   students who will page through us without ever under-
      standing who we were, or why
Blue of our sorrow, blue of our lust, blue of our anger,
   blue of our drowned desires
We will be (forever) our blue names.

ZOO

Which is the shortest way to the zoo?
This way? Around the corner? That way?
I ask a busdriver, he doesn't know.
I ask a short man whose breath smells of garlic.
He shakes his head. A zoo? In this town?
I walked and walked, and found a girl with long hair—
her green eyes were immense, mysterious.
She opened a zipper in her belly
and let me in. "This is the way," she said.
And it was.
Llamas! Sea lions! Camels! Orangutans!
Swift porpoises that know the secrets of the ocean!
An african vulture that has murdered in the sky!
"Is it safe?" she asked, leaning on my arm.
We fed peanuts to the elephants, threw fish
to the alligators. She opened the zipper again
and let me out.

I went home and slept, and dreamed
about the alligators.
A zipper at the edge of my dream
opened slowly. In the darkness beyond the zipper
I saw the green glow of her eyes. We stared
and stared. I moved toward her,
but the zipper closed. I walked for a while
along a narrow street, past a row of old houses.
All the houses were boarded up.
"Where's the zoo?" I asked a blind man, whose mouth
reeked of garlic. He shook his head. A zoo?
In this town?

PART TWO

WARM DAYS, NIGHTS OF GREEN LIGHTNING

WARM DAYS, NIGHTS OF GREEN LIGHTNING

The days are warm, the nights shimmer with green lightning.
I like the lightning, even when it's pink.
Low tenements rise from the ground like square thumbs.
My eyes get lost among the clotheslines.
It's Tuesday—eggs & sausages. "Eat," my mother says.
"Eat up! Eat up!" For as long as I can remember,
she's giving me food. The Italian fruitman
sells strawberries from a wagon. The cutlery man
grinds my mother's scissors. Fat old ladies
hang from the clotheslines by their toes.
These slow months, these languid days—I slip off
into my moods, my green confusions. Waiting.
Listening. Is this a stone? A bush? A cloud?
Is this a tree?

Thousands of ants swarm in the driveway, I count them.
My father pours alcohol over them and lights a match.
The little burnt ants smell like supper.
My father spins his arms like propellers
and flies above the clotheslines.
How he rises, soars, goes off!
The fat old ladies look on, look on—
and now they sing to him
with big vermilion mouths.

Vermilion! I discover vermilion!
This old 2¢ stamp is vermilion.
This 5:30 sky is vermilion.
These chapped hands are vermilion.
And these old ladies: their mouths! their mouths!

Somewhere a war is happening. A picture of my uncle,
helmet in hand, ankle-deep in the mud of Belgium. Please
send a souvenir. Comes a bullet,
comes an iron cross. I take off
in a Flying Fortress: I am pilot & copilot,
tail-gunner, bombardier. Frankfurt burns.
Dresden burns. Out of a murky sky, guns blazing,
I am constantly approaching, the great
deliverer, the giver of death. These warm days,
these nights of green lightning—learning an old wisdom,
and more.

Leaves fall, I sweep them up. Birds perch
on telephone wires. My mother
bakes a blueberry pie. Her vermouth eyes
still hold me in her power.

I dip my hand in the holy water font
and talk to Jesus, who is drowsy in the tabernacle.
If I stop masturbating, will the war come to an end?
He doesn't answer. The lame sexton
drags across the sanctuary,
rubbing his nose.

It's time to move on, time to travel.
I'm with Sherlock Holmes,
facing death in Musgrave Manor. We escape
with minor injuries. It's not easy.
There are risks, complications. "Be brave," my father says.
My mother says: "Be one of the reliable ones."
Life thickens. I am Boris Karloff,
stranded in the Sahara with the Lost Patrol.
A bad desert to get lost in—I rave,
lose my mind. I carry a wooden cross up a sand dune
and am shot dead by a mob of Arabs.
"Be strong," my mother says. I try.
I practice.

Rain falls, I bury my father—
I put him in a cardboard box
and lower him into the ground.
And now I bury my mother—
I set her in a silver rocking chair
and let her rock back and forth forever.
Out of my father's grave there grows a purple iris.
On my mother's grave, there is a yellow rose.
My mother and my father are a rose and an iris.
They grow, and grow.

The war is over, the troops come home.
What other shadow waits behind the door?
Am I progressing toward some definite conclusion
waiting for me at the end of my life
in the shape of a crow?

Soon, soon, my microfilm days arrive.
I go into training for a career as a spy.
To prowl through the world, incognito,
collecting vital information—not for the CIA,
not for the NKVD, but my own man,
freelancing through gardens & cities, hiding in churches,
picking up clues—and then, after much
searching, much probing, having touched
some meanings, to close the case and slip off, unnoticed.
I take my chance, make my decision—
I go underground and photograph everything I see.

Silences of the moon. The drift of stars. Unknown galaxies.
Is this Venus? Mars? The plum tree gives no plums.
What news from Haifa? I remember clotheslines,
dead ants. A 2¢ stamp. The Italian fruitman
sells out to a supermarket. The cutlery man
retires to Florida. Old ladies in frayed sweaters
    sit motionless
behind closed windows. 1948 snow
        covers all.

PART THREE

THE RESURRECTION OF THE SNAILS

IT HAPPENS

It happens before you know it, a slow coming,
the way pears grow on trees, raspberries on bushes—
blossoms appear, the bees are busy; you look away,
and suddenly the fruit is ripe, waiting
for the picker's hand.

How it happens is what fascinates,
as much as the speed. It is not a clear occurrence, rational
and plain, translatable into mathematical accuracies—
not, to put it another way, like passing
through the electronic doors in supermarkets,
the foot on the mat touching a switch you know is there,
a good clean connection making the door swing alertly open—
more intricate than that,
more mystifying, like arriving at an airport
and waiting for a delayed flight, then waking, unshaved,
bewildered, in another part of the world
where the language is unfamiliar.

Astonishment does not erase the fact—the event itself,
so glib and terrifying.
                              It happens.

RIDING WITH PANCHO VILLA

Pancho Villa rides into town—
   Kill! Kill!
It's love, death, passion, and misery,
the great green hope of the revolution.
Death to the gringos! Death to the priest!
Death to the would-be assassin!
We poison the wells and ride out.
They stab the great man in his left thigh & he bleeds
   forever, forever—
and then recovers
         goes on to accomplish great things.
He cannot read and cannot write—it is, he says,
   like being blind.
General Pershing sends
a message: EVERY GREAT MAN WAS ONCE A BANDIT!
And so we ride,
past shacks and adobe huts, cactus, gulches, ravines,
and still we ride,
and at the end of the dusty brown road
   on which we choke, & sweat, & hope, & search, & suffer,
   & make love, & lose our minds,
we find at last, under a hot sun, the small astounding death
            that we were looking for.

VERMEER

Vermeer van Delft: he paints
a different kind of poetry—reportorial,
exact. A maid pouring milk
into a bowl, bread on the table, light
coming through the window. A street
in Delft, every brick counted. Girls
playing lutes, guitars, virginals. A woman
reading a letter by a window, her reflection
grieving in the glass.
                        This realism is insistent,
it makes itself heard. Bodies always dressed,
hands busy, ears listening,
eyes containing whole worlds. Here
there are no nightmares; the only agonies
are those of the calendar, the continuing day:
quiet, inevitable.

TRANSFORMATIONS / THE SNAKE
LEAVES A NOTE

The bird breaks, and out of the bird
crawls a caterpillar. The caterpillar breaks,
and out of the caterpillar comes an orangutan.
The orangutan breaks, and out of the orangutan steps a camel.
The camel breaks, and out of the camel marches
a World War II nazi war criminal. The war criminal breaks,
and out walks a nun. The nun breaks, and out of the nun
flies an owl. The owl soars to the topmost
branches of a willow, saying: "I AM THE BIRD OF
THE BEGINNING AND THE END, THE BIRD
OF MYSTERY, THE BIRD OF SORROW AND DEATH—
FEAR ME!" The owl breaks,
and out of the owl comes a snake that says
nothing at all. The snake has
blue skin and yellow eyes: it lives for ninety-nine years,
eating, breeding, sleeping, dreaming,
planning. The snake keeps its silence,
never talks. When it dies, it leaves
a note scrawled in pencil: "I was there all the time,
and still am. Even though you don't see me, I am
alive & well, living in
unimaginable places. I shall return!"
The dead snake turns into a magician.
The magician performs a few tricks, then snaps
his fingers and disappears. All that remains

is the magician's voice, saying: "Now that my body has
vanished, who shall I be?" The magician's voice
turns into an exotic bird with flamboyant
yellow plumage. The bird flies off, higher and higher,
enters a cloud. The cloud disintegrates into rain.
The rain becomes flowers. The flowers die,
covered by snow. Nothing moves.
The landscape lies white and frozen, touched only
by the wind—waiting for a clue, a signal, fresh start,
alchemy, entelechy, an authentic
(undisguised) beginning.

GOODBYE

My father lies in a hospital bed
with fourteen tubes in his body.
All those treacherous liquids
flowing in and out of him! He opens
one eye, and in that black pool I see
all the flat tires he ever had on the road.

He smiles, and one by one removes
the tubes. His lips peel back
over yellow teeth—and now (slyly!) he stands.
Fluids gush from the holes in his body.
He is a walking fountain, making his way
to the toilet.

I wait a long time, noticing
my shoes are wet. When he returns, his fluids
are all gone—he's a shriveled almond.
I set him on the bed and hook up his tubes.
"Gently," he warns. These useless tubes,
they are dry twigs stripped of all their leaves.

Both of his eyes are open now—dark,
cheerless orbs. There are carnations
beside the bed; fondly, he touches one.
His sex rises, a stiff neon rod,
giving off an orange glow. The flat tires in his eyes
roll backwards into his past.

"Goodbye," he whispers—a low,
rust-filled sound. The orange glow
dies away. I take
the carnations
and spread them over his body. And now
I close his eyes.

WORKING AT THE EDGE

We are working at the edge. The edge
is not always generous, the edge is sometimes grey.
We have seen the edge on bad days,
   an edge is an edge.
There are times when the edge is dangerous,
we go home with bruises.

There is no velvet at the edge,
no smooth surfaces.
We hate the edge and spit on it, telling it
in no uncertain terms
that we would do without it if we could.

One day the edge went away, saying:
   "I am tired of being the edge—tired of
   being kicked, cursed, gouged, and pounded!"
The edge was gone for 3 days, then it came back.

No flowers grow at the edge, there are no trees.
Some of us die there.
The light is sometimes red, sometimes indigo,
the moon never rises.
Weekends, away from the edge, we wonder:
   What if the edge should go away forever?
   What if it should disappear?

We talk to the edge, needing it as it needs us.
Edge of our sorrow, edge of our memories,
edge of our dim beginnings.
Edge of our desperation and our emptiness.
Edge of our wages, our daily bread.

The edge is not holy, sane, or kind.
It pays back curse for curse.
Yet we labor there, and labor there,
the edge is what we know.

DESTROYER

The anchor pulls away from the muddy bottom.
　　There is movement again: the engines
have their way, the hull divides the water.
　　Who can fathom the meaning of the sea? Who
can separate its violence from its generative
　　powers? The way it takes the body of
a sailor, and with cold meticulousness transforms
　　his flesh into subtle organisms, food for
asterids, food for chimaeroids. The destroyer
　　moves into position in the fleet. The guns
are oiled and ready. The radarscope scans
　　the waves, searching for an enemy. The dead
sailor enters another kind of life, drifting
　　casually: no anguish, and no remorse,
no recollection of the naval code, or of the shoes
　　　　　　he used to wear.

SOLID GEOMETRY

When I was fourteen I discovered
the subtle intricacies of the dodecahedron. I touched
a plaster model, a clever interconnection of surfaces.
The first girl I loved was like that—
not very clever, but interconnected,
with full breasts and ravishing thighs
I learned to take the measure of. She was tall,
with abundant brown hair, and she danced, she danced—
not like the second girl I loved, who was a sullen cube.

The second girl I loved had hair on her lip
and warts on her shoulders—but her lines were simple,
she was solid and true.
And such power in her dreams!—
   a palm tree growing in a sea of blue milk,
    and a sea monster, massive, black, washed ashore
      on a deserted beach.
She was a world of potent meanings, too rich to last.

At sixteen I was a dreamer, pondering the calculus
of the perfect sphere. It hung before me, unattainable,
   drifting coyly in a celery sky.
I climbed a ladder, but it was no use—
perfect spheres were for larger souls than mine.
I returned to solid ground
and, at twenty, took up with a rhombohedron.
She was short and uncomplicated, with a straight nose
   and appleseed eyes—
   good legs, good arms, good teeth, and a firm bite
and she never let go.

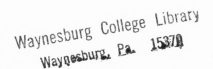

CONSUMER

I shave my beard and put on new clothes.
My newest disguise: I'm a consumer.
I eat everything in sight—nails, rugs, acorns.
Stay out of my reach. Land: I gobble it up.

What I don't eat, I wear—a sealskin vest,
an alligator belt. My ties are woven from llama wool.
A rabbit's foot hangs
from my cadmium watch chain.

My house is made of tinted glass—
tortoise shells for ashtrays,
panther pelts on the walls. I burn mahogany
in the fireplace.

Shopping at the deli: stuffed parrots,
    fried hippopotamus testicles, larks soaked in honey.
Look for me in the *New York Times*,
I'm the man in the centerfold, with one gold eye.

PANTOUM OF THE BROKEN RIVER

We dream of alligators and a river,
snails in swamps, starfish buried deep.
Is this the madness of a raging fever?
Are there meanings here that we can keep?

Snails in swamps, starfish buried deep—
who can solve the darkness of their death?
We find no meanings here that we can keep.
Time waits, grey memories are what we breathe.

Who can solve the awkwardness of death—
the hurt, the anguish, the lasting silence?
Time waits, grey memories are what we breathe.
We see the world through an unfocused lens.

The hurt, the terror, and enduring silence—
it is not easy to interpret pain.
We see the world through an unfocused lens.
The snails are covered by a purple rain.

It is not easy to account for pain
or purge the madness of our raging fever.
The snails are dying in a purple rain,
we dream of alligators and a river.

EVA

Virna Lisi is undressing on *The Late Show*.
The man in a tuxedo scowls at the man in a sport shirt:
"Get this clear," he says, "that girl is mine."
The man in a sport shirt doesn't seem to care.
He smiles, shrugs—knows she will be his.
I go to the kitchen for a bag of potato chips.
The refrigerator hums and leaks its little puddle.

That Virna Lisi—what a broad!
If I were the man in a sport shirt, I would want her too.
Seduced when she was eleven, she says. Who wouldn't
believe it! The mouth, the eyes, her moody silences . . .
The man in a sport shirt follows her home.
Her bare foot caresses his chin.
Their bodies come together.
Such heavy breathing!

Later, they are in a swank bar—
dim lights, bongo drums, a male dancer performing solo.
Virna Lisi is cool behind her dark glasses.
"Do you have enough money," she wants to know.
Her pearl necklace gleams between her teeth.
I wonder what a real pearl tastes like. Clams? Oysters?
Caviar?

They leave the bar, drive off.
Suddenly they are in a deserted mansion, going upstairs.
"What do you hate most?" he asks.
Her voice is cold enamel: "Apart from men? Old women."
He laughs—sharp, brittle laughter, echoing hideously.

Now they are in her room. He is despondent, sobbing.
"I stole my dead brother's soul," he confesses.
She is all affection—
she gives herself to him with her clothes on.
Afterwards, though, there is no real happiness.
"Get out!" she cries. "I told you not to fall in love with me!"

I go to the kitchen for more potato chips.
When I come back, they are enjoying themselves in Venice.
Gondolas! Pigeons! Accordions! At the bar
they drink Vat 69. But now
she turns him out: "I want to be paid," she says. "Cash!"
She lights a cigarette. She's in her pajamas again,
and sleeps alone.

A dark day, everyone is in black—
the wronged wife has committed suicide.
A gondola funeral.
Afterwards, Virna Lisi undresses again in her bedroom.
He watches through the window.
He breaks in, his hands are upon her.
She wrestles free, and drives him off with a whip.
The scars on his face look bad.

And now she is in the piazza, passing out icy goodbyes.
He stumbles along drunkenly.
"Will you see me when you come back?" he asks.
"Maybe," she says, turning away. "*If* I come back."
O that Virna Lisi, her face is as mean as stone.

THE LIP

I found a lip on the table
and didn't know
                        whose lip it was
—a thick lip, dark purple,
lying on the white formica
near an empty cup.

The lip smiled,
    then the smile went away.
The lip seemed about to talk—
it said nothing.

The lip stayed for seven days,
then disappeared.

I remember the lip because it was
    firm, definite, sure of itself, and unashamed:
a lip that knew how to appear and disappear
        when it wanted.

A photograph shows a small scar
where the lip was hit once by a stone.
Another photograph shows the lip
in a state of confusion: annoyed
    by a persistent fly.

The lip never communicated its thoughts—
never sang, never made a sound.
When it moved, it moved gracefully.

It was not the lip of doom,
or the lip of loss,
or the lip of eternally irreconcilable attitudes.

Sometimes the lip seemed about to whistle,
sometimes it seemed to have something very urgent
  it wanted to say.

It departed in the middle of the night,
leaving no sign that it would ever
come back.

BENJAMIN FRANKLIN SEEN AS A KITE
IN THE SKY OVER CONNECTICUT

Benjamin Franklin, what can I do? Give you a moustache?
Your small black eyes (black as in a lithograph) are sharp
  like sharpened pencils.
Life has its limits—no chance of rescuing you
  from venery, intemperance, gout, or common sense.
You go your own way, it's what you are.

I spray you with red paint and set you out to dry.
You stand among the rhododendrons, clever as ever,
  gossiping with the butterflies.
A stenographer takes down your words—
something about thrift, and something about flatulence,
  the influence of oil on troubled waters.
Your spectacles ride down your nose.
But how can I be of service? Offer you a dream?
I tie you to a string and let you fly, dangerous
  in the clouds, to catch a bolt of lightning
                                        if you can.

ANDROSSI

On an autumn evening, when the rain is falling
ever so lightly, the phantom of a drizzle,
I walk through the park, on the path by the lake,
and find Androssi—

his face is scarred from the trouble he had in Ruanda.
His shoulders are stooped. He has one eye.
He spent nineteen years on a plantation,
dealing in rubber.
If his one good eye were put on a scale,
would it weigh heavily
with the evil he has seen
and done?

"So I killed a man in Ruanda," he says.
"It was necessary, there were reasons."
I stare at him intently—the scar on his forehead,
the horror of his ruined eye.

We are so unlike each other—yet in so many ways
we are similar, as if he and I were on opposite sides
of the same mirror, living out
each other's memories.
"We are what we are," he says, using a tone of voice
that is part sarcasm, part sorrow.
Then, lighting a cigarette, inhaling deeply:
"In Ruanda, you would have been me."

On an autumn evening, when the surface of the lake
is troubled by the rain, he lingers, enigmatic,
not to be trusted—in the rain, a tenuous drizzle.
Androssi?

THE BOX

And now you go into the box
which is named *Dracula Is Risen from the Dead*.
There is nobody else in this box
which is lined with black velvet:
not even Dracula, who is truly risen.
Inside the box you find apples and pomegranates,
if you want them,
and any scent you wish—cedar, pine, acacia.
And now you press a button in the box
that brings a country scene:
cows and barns, white steeples,
horses grazing . . .
or this other button
that brings a subway car.
It lasts a long time,
the box, the box
and all its subtle mysteries,
and now you press this button
that brings a waterfall: it falls and falls
and comes with a faint rainbow
for a slight extra fee.
And though Dracula may be risen,
you are not:
you press the buttons in the box,

looking for the one
that will take you home—
but the box, the box
is always a box,
and the memories you never wanted,
locked doors, stalled elevators,
phone booths on winter nights,
have a way of lasting, a way
of holding: they will not
disappear. This button?
That? This other one?
The box.

MUSEUM

This stone pharaoh with a weatherworn face
knows more about power than about love—
his tapered body rises
from a hot pool of acid
boiling somewhere underground.
His mouth, what is left of it,
is all discipline, too stern to talk.

These Ming dragons are something else,
moiling and garrulous, with bulging red eyes.
Malevolent tongues spill from their open jaws.
They are all noise,
babbling in a strange language
about an ancient evil.

I pass into another room
and find a naked Venus on a pedestal.
Her marble thighs swell voluptuously.
My groin feels an old lechery
from a few thousand years ago,
and I have to get out of here,
onto the sidewalk,
where the girls wear false eyelashes
and green mascara,
and an old Greek with a moustache
sells pretzels
                    two for a quarter.

MONEY, LOSING ITS WAY IN A BLUE
FOREST OF DIMINISHING RETURNS

Money of sullen moods, troubled memories
Ducats, groats, florins, piasters
Money of Herculaneum and Pompeii, Charlemagne's denarius
    worth 1/240 of a pound of silver
Money in the form of beads, cows, sweet potatoes
In the form of apricots
Credit money, fiat money, managed money
Money of improbable long hair hanging down over the
    shoulders of Gina Lollobrigida
Of inkblot dreams, jungle phantasies, flickering electronic
    lightshows
Of the long sigh of Czarina Alexandra when she learns, a cold
    night in December, Rasputin is dead
Money of the 4 o'clock watercolor sky: today, now,
    bleak evanescence of dying turquoise, bandaged by
    brown clouds
Paper money invented by the Chinese, who invented
    gunpowder
Money like a decrepit clapboard house where an old man
    lived for a long time and then died—you wonder who this
        old man was, how much he suffered, was he familiar with
    Van Gogh, had he read Dostoevski, was he partial to
        Italian opera, was he consumed with passion for the wife
    of his best friend, was he concerned for the future of
        the blue whale, did he drink, did he worry, did he
    prefer walnuts to cashews, did he eat plums, did he grieve,
        did he agonize, did he die intestate . . .

Money of swollen hopes and unimaginable blue-eyed
  daydreams, taped together, end to end, forming
  unlikely interstate highways that twist
    & turn & go clear across to California
Money singing, doing the dance of the dollar in topless
  casinos in Las Vegas, growing like mangos in Florida,
  pecans in Georgia, stretching out like desert sand
    in Nevada
Examined under microscopes in corporation laboratories
  & found to be lefthanded, hunchbacked, crosseyed, green
Money is limping along, doing its best to abide by Irving
  Fisher's formula for the flow of money: $MV + M'V' = PT$
Money of devious ways and subtle purposes, passing in & out
  of dim rooms, unlocking doors, filmed in techni-
  color in roadside motels all over America and declared
    by the U.S. Supreme Court to be obscene
Money of Solomon, Rameses II, Tamburlaine, David
  Rockefeller
Of Sabah Al-Salim Al-Sabah
Of Howard Hughes in a purple bathrobe, eating snails
Of Chingachgook, the very last of the Mohicans,
  who died poor
Of George Sanders swallowing an overdose of sleeping pills in
  Castelldefels, Spain—"Dear World: I am leaving because I
  am bored. I feel I have lived long enough. I am leaving
  you with your worries in this sweet cesspool—good luck."
Money of the great emptiness, the lost beyond, sinking like
  desperate Spanish galleons in the Gulf of Mexico
Money of parched lips and slow, inordinate ecstasies: rupees,
  dinars, guilders, pesos, kroner, quetzales, yen

Colonial money of North Carolina bearing the inexorable
    motto: "American Virtue Triumphant"
Money like whole herds of bison shot dead by Buffalo Bill
The Grand Canyon as money, the Petrified Forest, Pike's Peak,
    Niagara Falls
Money making its way, stumbling along, crossing buttes
    & ravines, arriving on the west coast like Balboa dis-
    covering the Pacific
Money as the comet Kohoutek, disappointment of the century,
    fading fast, vanishing, heading for greener pastures in
    another part of the universe
It's a bad time for money, the wrong season and wrong year
In New Orleans they're playing the blues for money
At Lincoln Center they're performing Verdi's *Requiem*
It's a five-hundred-car funeral, with flowers sent from all
    over the world—Malaysia, Afghanistan, Outer Mongolia,
    Madagascar
They're digging a big hole for money, burying it deep
In Forest Lawn, money is biding its time, resting, waiting,
    making plans for a big resurrection, the moment of trans-
    figuration when it will reappear in the form of Aurora
    Borealis: phantasmagoric rose/yellow/blue, flashing,
    shimmering, seen only in the right place, at the right
    time, and always (permanently) out of reach.

LAST DAYS IN MARRAKECH

We have all gathered here—Sakkos who makes films,
Mraz who sells bonds, and my friend Katz
who programs computers. Time passes slowly.
The days thicken, growing like fruit
toward some unforeseen ripening.

"Is this Marrakech?" Sakkos wonders. "Why have we come
to Marrakech?" The sun beats down,
burning the grass. It is always Marrakech,
a distant place
in the mind. We have seen the cork trees,
and the mines where they dig manganese.
We found the almonds, the figs, the plums.
Sakkos says again: "Why have we come?"

We live in a whitewashed cottage where, last month,
an old man died. What difference can it make?
One dies young, another dies old.
We are always dead (as Katz is fond of saying)
even before we are born.

Sakkos died in bed with a woman—he never knew
her name. Mraz died in a hospital, surrounded by
his seven children. Katz, a halfhearted agnostic,
died in a synagogue.

Sakkos calls for more gin. I go to the house
and bring out another bottle.
A sudden wind tears at the trees.
The leaves are green and tough—
they will hold.

We drink away the afternoon, and when the sun goes down
we walk, uncertainly, through an open window
toward an old sorrow
waiting for us in the auburn sky.
Nothing matters now. We are making our way,
as we must.

MERLIN SITS AT THE EDGE OF
THE ROAD, EXPECTING THE WORST

Take and lose, soft and remember: we will never know
how (or why) we began. Trees break loose
and sail off in the wind. Clouds hug the ground.
Birds fly through open windows. We wait
for meaning to take hold.

A blue fox sits near a
crooked tree. A purple horse
rages across a ploughed field. A red
crow flies through a narrow cloud. A dead fish
dreams on the silver grass. A tired hound sleeps
in an amber house. A menacing eye leans down out of
the sky.

Why do these lilacs wait & wait? Will green
meanings push through, at last, like grass?

THE RESURRECTION OF THE SNAILS

This is the resurrection of all the dead snails
    witnessed in a dream by a girl in Managua
and a boy in Porto-Novo
    and by an old woman who was dying of a fever
in Dar es Salaam . . . a resurrection that occurred
    in dreams all over the world, in different
time zones, while rain was falling on the homes
    of the dreamers, and pink glimmers of lightning
were flickering in the sky. The snails come forth,
    cepaea nemoralis, belgrandia marginata,
emerging from the slime of their graves
    with resolve, determination: a slow advance
accompanied by triumphal music,
    tabors & fifes, trumpets, bass drums—
they arrive and arrive, snails by the millions,
    crowding into Wall Street, swarming over Manhattan,
inhabiting the restaurants and the air-cooled offices:
    because this
is their resurrection, the inheritance
    they have yearned for—the brown sky
and the smokestacks, and the glass skyscrapers,
    promised to them from generation to generation.
They are moving in, taking possession.
    It was revealed in a dream in Managua, and in a dream
in Porto-Novo, and it was told over and over again
    to an old woman in Dar es Salaam
who was dying of a fever. The snails, the snails—
    they know what is theirs, & will not be denied.